CIVIL RIGHTS DIVISION HIGHLIGHTS: 2009 – 2017

Fulfilling America's Promise of Equal Justice and Equal Opportunity for All

January 2017

Dear Colleagues and Stakeholders:

For nearly six decades, through the zigs and zags of our nation's history, the career men and women of the Civil Rights Division have worked tirelessly to advance justice and ensure equality. In so doing, they have helped transform our nation into a more just, more inclusive and more perfect union. During the last eight years, under the leadership of President Barack Obama, Attorney General Eric Holder and Attorney General Loretta E. Lynch, the division has continued to play a forceful and pivotal role in advancing this vision. Our work has made a tangible difference in the lives of countless individuals across the country.

From policing and criminal justice reform to LGBT rights and voting, the division has fought discriminatory barriers and opened doors of opportunity for some of the most vulnerable among us, including people with disabilities, people of color, people living in poverty and people who speak English as a second language. This document provides an overview of key accomplishments and highlights from our work over the past eight years. It does not summarize every case brought or every brief filed. Rather, this document aims to convey a holistic story about the impact and scope of the division's efforts during the Obama Administration.

Beyond the concrete achievements detailed in the enclosed headlines, there are, of course, other less tangible, but equally important, aspects of our work. By ensuring constitutional policing, the division has worked to advance public safety and strengthen the relationships between law enforcement and the communities they serve. In LGBT rights, in cases on marriage equality and transgender rights, we have made historic statements not only about legal protections but also about human dignity. And in voting rights, even with the setback of *Shelby County v. Holder*, the division has continued to vigorously enforce the remaining tools at our disposal, ensuring that eligible voters get to participate in the electoral process with the ease and access that federal law guarantees. The legacy of these efforts will live on for generations to come.

To me, our work has always been about more than just winning cases. In a broader sense, it is about ensuring trust in public institutions to defend the legitimacy of our justice system and the integrity of our democracy. Over the last two plus years, I have had the privilege to work alongside a team of outstanding colleagues. I know they will continue to advance the division's mission of equal justice, equal opportunity and equal protection for all with steadfast determination and keen focus on the people who count on us each day to make government deliver results and vindicate rights in their communities.

Sincerely,

Vanita Gupta

Principal Deputy Assistant Attorney General
Civil Rights Division, U.S. Department of Justice

TABLE OF CONTENTS

Protected Disability Rights 4

Fought Religious Discrimination 8

Worked to Fulfill the Promise of Equal Educational Opportunity For All 10

Advanced Economic Opportunity by Ensuring Equal Access to Credit 13

Enforced the Fair Housing Act 15

Defended the Rights of Servicemembers 17

Protected the Civil Rights of LGBT Women, Men and Children 19

Fought Discrimination and Expanded Equal Opportunity in the Workplace 23

Advanced Constitutional Policing 27

Prosecuted Criminal Law Enforcement Misconduct 32

Prosecuted Human Trafficking 34

Prosecuted Hate Crimes 36

Protected Access to Reproductive Health Care 38

Defended the Bedrock of Our Democracy – The Right to Vote 39

Promoted Access to Justice 42

Advanced Juvenile Justice Reform 44

Reformed Restrictive Housing and Corrections Practices 46

Protected the Rights of Limited English Proficient (LEP) Individuals and Prevented
National Origin and Racial Discrimination by Recipients of Federal Funds 48

Resources 51

PROTECTED DISABILITY RIGHTS

Not long ago, for people with disabilities, America's dream and promise of equal opportunity felt distant and out of reach. Yet over time, advocacy drove legal change. And legal change led to lives transformed, futures reclaimed and dreams restored. Congress passed the Rehabilitation Act in 1973 and then the Americans with Disabilities Act (ADA) in 1990. The ADA ushered in a new era for people with disabilities in this country. Progress built the pathway for further reform. And in 1999, in *Olmstead v. L.C.*, the Supreme Court enunciated a crucial tenet of the ADA: the community integration mandate. The court held that under the ADA, "unjustified institutional isolation of persons with disabilities" constitutes discrimination. Because of the division's *Olmstead* work, today more than 53,000 people with disabilities will have meaningful opportunities to receive services in integrated, community-based settings. In other areas, too, from transportation, to education, to voting, the division has worked tirelessly to ensure that all people can live with independence, with dignity and with full inclusion in the mainstream of American life.

Reached Landmark Settlement with State of Oregon Regarding ADA and Sheltered Workshops. In December 2015, a federal court approved a settlement agreement between the division, a class of private plaintiffs and the state of Oregon, which resolved the division's and the class plaintiffs' claims against the state under the ADA. The agreement will impact approximately 7,000 Oregonians with intellectual and developmental disabilities who can and want to work in typical employment settings in the community. The settlement resolved the first class action lawsuit in the nation to challenge a state funded and administered employment service system that unnecessarily placed people in sheltered workshops, as a violation of the ADA's integration mandate.

> Today, Zavier no longer earns $1.70 per hour assembling small company parts. Instead, with employment support, he works at a local YMCA, helping kids complete their homework and resolve their conflicts.

Reached Settlements to Ensure that Thousands of Rhode Islanders with Disabilities Can Work in Competitive, Integrated Employment. Following investigations of Rhode Island's employment service system, in 2013 and 2014, respectively, the division reached an interim settlement agreement with Rhode Island and the city of Providence, and a statewide consent decree with Rhode Island. The statewide consent decree will provide relief to approximately 3,250 people in, or at risk of entry into, segregated sheltered workshops. The consent decree will ensure that, over the next decade, approximately 2,000 Rhode Islanders with disabilities will have the opportunity to work in competitive integrated employment, and approximately 1,250 students with disabilities will get the services they need to transition into the competitive workforce.

Issued ADA Technical Assistance. Building on its work in Rhode Island and Oregon, the division also issued technical assistance explaining how state employment service systems can comply with the ADA and *Olmstead*.

> The division has answered more than **415,300** calls to the ADA Information Line to assist callers in applying the ADA to their own unique situations. The ADA.gov website got **233 million** hits.

Sued Georgia for Unnecessarily Segregating Students with Disabilities. In August 2016, the division filed a lawsuit against the state of Georgia alleging that its treatment and segregation of nearly 5,000 students with disabilities in the Georgia Network for Educational and Therapeutic Support (GNETS) Program violates the ADA. The lawsuit alleges that Georgia's administration of its mental health and therapeutic educational services for students with behavior-related disabilities unnecessarily segregates students with disabilities in GNETS when they could appropriately be served with their peers in general education settings. The lawsuit is the first challenge to a state-run school system for segregating students with disabilities.

Prioritized Appropriate Diversion of Individuals with Disabilities from the Criminal Justice System. The division placed a high priority on preventing needless criminal justice involvement of individuals with disabilities. This work led to the inclusion of an ADA claim in the August 2016 Baltimore City Police Department findings letter; inclusion of relief focused on diversion in a corrections settlement agreement with Hinds County, Mississippi; and a lawsuit challenging the state of Mississippi's failure to provide sufficient mental health services in the community.

Fostered Successful Reform of Delaware Service System for People with Mental Illness. In October 2016, a federal court terminated the remedial settlement agreement governing the state of Delaware's service system for people with serious and persistent mental illness. The state significantly expanded and enhanced community-based mental health services for individuals with serious and persistent mental illness under the agreement, as required by the ADA and the Supreme Court's *Olmstead* decision.

Found West Virginia's Children's Mental Health System Violates the ADA. In June 2015, the division released its findings that West Virginia institutionalizes over 1,000 children in segregated, residential facilities when many of them could be served in the community. The letter found that certain children were at heighted risk of institutional placement, including racial minorities, trauma-exposed children and LGBT children.

Found South Dakota Unnecessarily Relies on Nursing Facilities to Provide Services to People with Disabilities. Following a comprehensive investigation, in May 2016 the division released its findings that South Dakota unnecessarily relies on nursing facilities to provide services to people with disabilities, in violation of the community integration mandate of the ADA and the

Supreme Court's *Olmstead* decision. South Dakotans with disabilities do not have a meaningful choice to receive the services they need in their own homes and communities.

Reached ADA Settlement with Wells Fargo. In May 2011, the division announced a comprehensive settlement agreement under the ADA with Wells Fargo & Company to ensure equal access for individuals with disabilities to Wells Fargo's services nationwide, including its nearly 10,000 retail banking, brokerage and mortgage stores; over 12,000 ATMs; and its telephone and website services. Under the agreement, Wells Fargo has paid a total of almost $15.2 million to 925 people who experienced discrimination in banking in violation of the ADA – the largest payment under an ADA settlement with the Justice Department.

Settled Lawsuit Alleging Discrimination by Large Network of Private Schools Against Children with Disabilities for $215,000. In January 2011, Nobel Learning Communities Inc. (NLC), which operates a network of more than 180 preschools, elementary schools and secondary schools in 16 states throughout the country, entered into a settlement agreement to resolve the division's lawsuit alleging that NLC violated the ADA by excluding children with autism spectrum disorders and other disabilities from its programs.

Reached Settlement with Greyhound Lines to Resolve ADA Violations. In February 2016, as part of a settlement agreement reached with the division, Greyhound Lines Inc. – the nation's largest provider of intercity bus transportation – agreed to implement a series of systemic reforms to resolve allegations that it repeatedly violated the ADA. Under the terms of the agreement, Greyhound, which serves more than 3,800 destinations and more than 18 million passengers each year across North America, will compensate several classes of passengers who faced barriers because of their disabilities.

Reached Agreement to Remedy ADA Violations by Carnival Cruise Line, Holland America Line and Princess Cruises. The division and Carnival Corporation – one of the largest cruise companies in the world – reached a comprehensive, landmark settlement agreement under the ADA to advance equal access for individuals with disabilities who travel on cruise ships.

Launched Barrier-Free Health Care Initiative. Through the Barrier-Free Health Care Initiative, U.S. Attorneys across the nation partnered with the division to ensure that people with disabilities, including those who are deaf or have hearing loss, have access to medical care. The initiative has included investigations and settlements with a large array of health care providers, including nursing facilities, dentists, doctors, hospitals, pharmacies and mental health facilities. In one case, in September 2013, the division reached a $55,000 settlement under the ADA with Dominion Hospital, a psychiatric facility in Falls Church, Virginia, to ensure effective communication with people who have hearing disabilities in the provision of medical services.

Reached Settlement with South Carolina Department of Corrections to End Discrimination Against Inmates with HIV. The division reached a settlement with the South Carolina Department of Corrections (SCDC) to resolve alleged violations of Title II of the ADA and Section 504 of the Rehabilitation Act of 1973. The agreement resolved the division's investigation of SCDC's practice of segregating inmates with HIV/AIDS and denying them the opportunity to participate equally in services, programs and activities.

Reached Agreement with Robeson County, North Carolina, to Increase Accessibility. In July 2015, Robeson County, North Carolina, and the division reached an agreement under which the county – which is geographically the largest and poorest county in North Carolina and nearly 40 percent Native American – is continuing its work to bring two of its playgrounds into compliance with current ADA standards so that children with disabilities can play there, alongside children without disabilities. This agreement is part of Project Civic Access (PCA), the division's initiative to ensure that cities, towns and counties throughout the country comply with the ADA. The division has reached 63 PCA agreements since 2009.

Reached Agreement with Nueces County, Texas, to Improve Accessibility of Services and Programs. In January 2015, the division reached an agreement with Nueces County, Texas, that requires the county to assess all existing web content and online services for conformance with industry guidelines – the Web Content Accessibility Guidelines (WCAG) 2.0 – to make web content accessible. Under the agreement, Nueces County will also ensure that people with disabilities – especially people who use wheelchairs and other mobility devices – can get inside buildings that offer county services and programs.

Reached ADA Agreements to Make Technology Accessible. The division reached agreements with edX Inc., Louisiana Tech University, Peapod and others to make online information and technologies accessible to people with disabilities.

Published Final Rules Incorporating the ADA Amendments Act. In September 2010, the division published two final rules to amend its ADA Title II and Title III regulations to update the definition of disability under the ADA Amendments Act. The regulations apply to the activities of more than 80,000 units of state and local government and more than 7 million places of public accommodation, including stores, restaurants, shopping malls, libraries, museums, sporting arenas, movie theaters, doctors' and dentists' offices, hotels, jails and prisons, polling places and emergency preparedness shelters.

Published a Final Rule on ADA Requirements for Movie Theaters. In November 2016, the division published a final rule under Title III of the ADA to require movie theaters to exhibit closed movie captioning and audio description when exhibiting movies that have those features.

FOUGHT RELIGIOUS DISCRIMINATION

In communities around the country today, many people of various faiths, beliefs and backgrounds endure threats or discrimination because of the religion they practice or their place of worship. Whether prosecuting religion-based hate crimes or combating religious discrimination in education, employment and land use, the division leads a wide range of enforcement actions to protect religious freedom for all. Following heinous terrorist attacks in recent months, Muslim communities, and others perceived to be Muslim, continue to suffer a particularly notable backlash. This discriminatory backlash doesn't just harm one community. It violates the defining values of our country. And it threatens all of us who call America home. The division works aggressively to defend the rights of every person to live free from violence, harassment and discrimination – rights that our Constitution guarantees and rights that form the bedrock of a free, open and inclusive society.

Prosecuted Religion-based Hate Crimes. The division, in partnership with U.S. Attorneys' Offices, prosecuted dozens of religion-based hate crimes around the country. Recent cases include convicting a Connecticut man for firing a high-powered rifle at a mosque; a Florida man for threatening to firebomb two mosques and shoot their congregants; a former Missouri man for leading a conspiracy to deface a local Islamic Center with graffiti and burn two copies of the Quran; a Missouri man for the arson of a local mosque and two attempted arsons of a Planned Parenthood clinic; a North Carolina man for using force against a Muslim woman to obstruct her free exercise of religion on an airplane; and a Minnesota man for obstructing, by threat of force, the free exercise of religious beliefs when he wrote and mailed a threatening letter to an Islamic Center. In recent years, the division also prosecuted defendants for beating a Sikh cab driver in Washington State, vandalizing churches in California and firing a gun at a synagogue in Utah.

Continued to Protect the Rights of Religious Communities to Build and Construct Places of Worship Free from Unlawful Barriers. In recent years, the division has increased its enforcement of the land use protections in the Religious Land Use and Institutionalized Persons Act (RLUIPA), which protects religious communities from discriminatory or unjustifiably burdensome application of zoning laws against places of worship, religious schools and other uses of land for religious purposes. For the period from 2010 to the present, RLUIPA investigations per year rose 60 percent compared to the period from 2000 to 2010. RLUIPA cases brought per year increased by 160 percent. In 2016, the division filed suit against Bernards Township, New Jersey; Culpeper County, Virginia; and Sterling Heights, Michigan, for violating RLUIPA, alleging that the jurisdictions unlawfully blocked the construction of mosques. In December 2016, the division sent a letter to municipalities reminding them about RLUIPA's requirements.

Filed Lawsuit Requiring Rutherford County, Tennessee, to Allow Mosque to Open in City of Murfreesboro. The division filed suit under RLUIPA and won a temporary restraining order in federal court in Tennessee in July 2012 allowing the Islamic Center of Murfreesboro to move into a mosque it built on land that allows places of worship as of right. The division filed the suit in response to a state Chancery Court order blocking the county from issuing a certificate of occupancy in a suit brought by county residents who cited fears of terrorism, sharia law and related concerns.

Resolved Lawsuit with Pittsfield Charter Township Over Denial of Zoning Approval for Islamic School. In September 2016, the division announced a settlement with Pittsfield Charter Township, Michigan, resolving allegations that the township violated RLUIPA in denying zoning approval to allow the Michigan Islamic Academy (MIA) to build a school on a vacant parcel of land.

Launched New Community Engagement Initiative to Combat Religious Discrimination. In 2016, the Division launched *Combating Religious Discrimination Today*, a new interagency community engagement initiative designed to promote religious freedom, challenge religious discrimination and enhance enforcement of religion-based hate crimes. The division, in partnership with other federal agencies, hosted a series of community roundtables across the country that focused on protecting people and places of worship from religion-based hate crimes; combating religious discrimination, including bullying, in education and employment; and addressing unlawful barriers that interfere with the construction of places of worship. The division released a final report on the initiative in July 2016.

Government officials and community members discussed issues related to religious discrimination in employment at a roundtable held in Birmingham, Alabama, on April 20, 2016.

WORKED TO FULFILL THE PROMISE OF EQUAL EDUCATIONAL OPPORTUNITY FOR ALL

The division enforces federal laws designed to ensure equal educational opportunities for all of our nation's students. It enforces desegregation consent decrees to ensure that students of all races have equal access to resources and opportunities, particularly in the areas of qualified faculty and staff, facilities, extracurricular activities, transportation, student assignments and course offerings. It combats the school-to-prison pipeline and seeks to eliminate discriminatory discipline practices, which disproportionately harm children of color and children with disabilities. It ensures that English Learner (EL) students receive an education that meets their needs. It seeks equal educational opportunity for students with disabilities. And it resolves allegations of harassment based on race, national origin, religion, sex and disability in K-12 schools and institutions of higher education.

Federal Court Ordered Division's Desegregation Plan for Cleveland, Mississippi, Schools. In May 2016, following a five-decade-long legal battle to desegregate schools in Cleveland, Mississippi, a federal court ordered the Cleveland School District to consolidate its secondary schools. In spite of a 1969 court order mandating desegregation, there are two public school systems in Cleveland, where railroad tracks separate east from west and black from white. The court rejected as unconstitutional two alternatives proposed by the school district, agreeing with the division that the only way to achieve desegregation is by consolidating Cleveland's high schools and middle schools.

Reached Settlement with School District to Desegregate Elementary School Classrooms in Ruston, Louisiana. In June 2015, a federal court approved a court-ordered agreement with the Lincoln Parish School Board to desegregate classrooms at four elementary schools serving students in grades K-5 in Ruston, Louisiana. The division and the board jointly filed the consent order, after an investigation by the division found significant racial isolation in the elementary school classrooms (called "homerooms"). This consent decree, addressing *in-school* segregation, followed an earlier agreement that had required desegregation *across* Lincoln Parish's elementary schools.

Court Approved Consent Order to Further Desegregate and Address Racial Inequalities in Huntsville City Schools. In April 2015, a federal court approved a consent order filed by the division and the Huntsville City Schools to reconfigure school attendance zones, improve access to quality course offerings and address racial discrimination in student discipline, among other areas. In a 29-page opinion approving the consent order, U.S. District Judge Madeleine Hughes Haikala of the Northern District of Alabama called the plan a "game-changer" in the effort to finally eliminate the effects of state-mandated racial segregation in Huntsville.

Reached Voluntary Settlement with Arizona Department of Education to Meet the Needs of English Learner Students. In May 2016, the division, together with the U.S. Department of Education, entered into a settlement agreement with the Arizona Department of Education (ADE) that requires ADE to raise its English proficiency criteria to accurately identify EL students and to properly determine when EL students no longer need language services. The agreement also requires ADE to ensure that Arizona public schools offer language services to tens of thousands of students who were prematurely moved out of the EL program or incorrectly identified as fluent in English.

Reached Settlement to Ensure Equal Educational Opportunities for All English Learner Students in San Francisco. In June 2015, the division announced a comprehensive modified consent decree (now approved by the court) in the landmark case of *Lau v. Nichols*, in which the Supreme Court held that public schools must provide meaningful access to their educational programs for EL students. The consent decree requires the San Francisco Unified School District to provide language services to the more than 16,000 EL students enrolled in 110 schools.

Released Guidance to Ensure Equal Educational Opportunities for English Learner Students. In January 2015, the division and the U.S. Department of Education jointly released comprehensive guidance to remind state education agencies, school districts and public schools of their obligations under federal law to ensure that EL students have equal access to a high-quality education and the opportunity to achieve their full academic potential. The guidance animates the Supreme Court's *Lau v. Nichols* case and reminds states and schools of the ongoing importance in serving the approximately 5 million EL students in public schools in accordance with Title VI of the Civil Rights Act of 1964.

Reached Settlement with DeKalb County, Georgia, School District to Prevent Harassment Based on Religion and National Origin. In November 2014, the division reached a settlement agreement with the DeKalb County, Georgia, School District to resolve its inquiry into the district's response to peer-on-peer harassment based on national origin and religion. The agreement ensures that the more than 100,000 students in the school district will be protected by clear and comprehensive anti-harassment policies and procedures in compliance with federal civil rights laws.

Reached Agreements with Colleges and Universities to Protect Students from Sexual Harassment and Assault. In October 2016, the division and the U.S. Attorney's Office for the District of New Mexico reached an agreement with the University of New Mexico (UNM) to ensure that UNM responds swiftly and effectively to allegations of sexual harassment, including sexual assault, involving students. The agreement resolves the division's findings of UNM's non-compliance with Title IX of the Education Amendments of 1972 and Title IV of the Civil Rights Act of 1964. The division reached similar agreements with Wheaton College, in Massachusetts in September 2016, and with the University of Montana in May 2013.

Reached Settlement to Prevent and Address Racial Discrimination in Student Discipline in Meridian, Mississippi. In March 2013, the division reached a landmark consent decree with the Meridian, Mississippi, Public School District to prevent and address racial discrimination in student discipline in district schools. The consent decree resolves the division's investigation into complaints that the district unlawfully and disproportionately subjected African-American students to suspension, expulsion and school-based arrests, often for minor infractions such as violating the dress code by wearing the wrong color socks or leaving their shirts untucked.

Reached Settlement with School District of Palm Beach County, Florida, to Prevent and Address Discrimination in School Enrollment and Student Discipline. In February 2013, the division reached a settlement with the School District of Palm Beach County, Florida, the nation's 11th-largest school district, to prevent and address discrimination in school enrollment and student discipline. The division's investigation found that schools required EL students to comply with discipline policies that they couldn't understand. The settlement requires Palm Beach schools to make their discipline policies accessible to EL students and to communicate with parents about their student's behavior in a language that the parent understands. The district serves more than 179,000 students, including 20,000 EL students.

Filed Briefs Addressing the School-to-Prison Pipeline. The division has taken action to combat the school-to-prison pipeline, the cycle of harsh school discipline that brings young people into the justice system and disproportionately affects, among others, students of color and students with disabilities. For example, in October 2015, the division filed a statement of interest in *S.R. & L.G. v. Kenton County, et al.*, a case involving two elementary school children who allege that a school resource officer (SRO) violated their rights under the Constitution and Title II of the ADA when the SRO handcuffed them in school after the children exhibited conduct arising out of their disabilities. The brief explains the legal requirements to protect the rights of children in their interactions with SROs, describes the facts and circumstances the court should consider in evaluating whether the SRO's conduct in this case was constitutional and confirms that the ADA applies to SROs' interactions with children with disabilities. In November 2016, the division filed a Statement of Interest in *Kenny, et al v. Wilson, et al.*, articulating the United States' position that laws invoked to charge juveniles must include clear standards to ensure that they are enforced consistently and free from discrimination. The brief explains that "significant racial disparities in the enforcement of a criminal statute may indicate that the statute is unconstitutionally vague." It also asserts that laws that lack clear standards and do not provide sufficient guidance to law enforcement can lead to arbitrary or discriminatory enforcement.

Filed Amicus Brief in Landmark Diversity in Higher Education Case before the Supreme Court. The division worked on the Justice Department's amicus brief in *Fisher v. University of Texas at Austin,* in which the U.S. Supreme Court recognized the compelling interest in ensuring diversity in higher education. The department's brief argued that the university's limited consideration of race to achieve the educational benefits of diversity is constitutional because the university clearly defined its educational objectives and demonstrated that it had been unable to achieve the educational benefits of diversity without considering race in its holistic review analysis. Emphasizing the unique nature of the university's admissions program, the Supreme Court agreed in a June 2016 decision.

> **"Our country is stronger, more credible and more effective when our educational institutions include highly-qualified individuals with roots, cultures and traditions that reflect our nation's rich diversity."**
>
> *— Statement from Attorney General Loretta E. Lynch on the U.S. Supreme Court Ruling in Fisher v. University of Texas at Austin*

ADVANCED ECONOMIC OPPORTUNITY BY ENSURING EQUAL ACCESS TO CREDIT

In the American economy, credit serves as a key rung on the ladder of economic mobility. Credit enables working families to borrow money so they can buy a home, purchase a car, collect savings, start a business or finance an education. When some communities lack access to credit because of unlawful, discriminatory barriers – that means that some people don't get the same opportunities as others do to own property, to build equity and to increase wealth. Discriminatory lending results in lower property values, less investment, lost tax revenue and fewer jobs. The impact of those losses – stunted economic growth and diminished economic opportunity – hurts our economy and our country. In the aftermath of the Great Recession – which resulted, in part, from discriminatory, predatory lending practices – the division created a fair lending unit. Since 2010, in partnership with our U.S. Attorney colleagues, the division has obtained more than $1.6 billion in relief for individual victims, including nearly $460 million for servicemembers, and impacted communities.

Reached Settlement with BancorpSouth Bank to Resolve Allegations of Mortgage Lending Discrimination. In June 2016, the division and the Consumer Financial Protection Bureau (CFPB) filed a joint complaint and consent order involving BancorpSouth Bank for redlining – or denying someone credit because of where she or he lives – minority neighborhoods in the Memphis, Tennessee, area; discriminating in the underwriting of certain mortgage loans; discriminating in the pricing of certain mortgage loans; and implementing a policy that required its employees to treat loan applications differently based on the applicant's race or other prohibited characteristics. The allegations of this case demonstrate that minority borrowers continue to face a variety of hurdles at virtually every stage of the lending process, from how banks solicit applications to the discretion granted to loan officers and underwriters to approve and price the loans.

Reached Over $27 Million Settlement with Hudson City Savings Bank to Ensure Equal Lending Services to Predominantly Black and Hispanic Communities. In September 2015, the division and the CFPB filed a joint complaint and proposed consent order involving Hudson City Savings Bank alleging a pattern or practice of redlining throughout its major market areas in New Jersey, New York, Connecticut and Pennsylvania. Under the consent order, the bank agreed to provide $25 million in a loan subsidy fund to increase the amount of credit the bank extends to formerly redlined neighborhoods across its market areas; open two full-service branches in these neighborhoods and invest $2.25 million for advertising, outreach, financial education and community partnership efforts. This resolution represents the Justice Department's largest residential mortgage redlining settlement in its history.

Fought Discrimination in Auto Lending and Won Consumers $62 Million in Relief. To address discrimination in the financing of automobiles, the division and the CFPB settled three cases each alleging a pattern or practice of discrimination against many thousands of borrowers by indirect auto lenders. These cases alleged that American Honda Finance Corporation, Toyota Motor Credit Corporation and Fifth Third Bank permitted auto dealers to charge higher interest rates to minority borrowers. To resolve these cases, the lenders agreed to pay a total of at least $62 million to consumers and to limit dealer markup to levels that the agencies expect will significantly decrease discriminatory pricing disparities.

"Fair lending work … directly contributes to the founding promise of our democracy. In America, we don't guarantee equal outcomes. But we do promise equality of opportunity – the timeless American ideal that says if you work hard, if you play by the rules and if you follow the law, you deserve a fair shot and an equal chance to succeed."

– Head of the Civil Rights Division Vanita Gupta

ENFORCED THE FAIR HOUSING ACT

Housing discrimination limits economic opportunity. And diminished economic opportunity derails hope – hope that through the tenacity of work and the resiliency of spirit, people in this country can lift themselves up, invest in their dreams and seize the promise of a brighter future. Housing can affect where you get a job, the kind of school you attend, how you get to work and whether you live in a safe community. Almost five decades after the passage of the Fair Housing Act, housing discrimination and segregation continue to plague communities across the country. Far too many home seekers encounter prejudice, stereotypes, and discrimination that limit where they can live.

Won Religious Discrimination Lawsuit Against Colorado City, Arizona, and Hildale, Utah. In March 2016, a federal jury returned a verdict finding that the towns of Colorado City, Arizona, and Hildale, Utah, and their joint water company systematically discriminated against individuals who are not members of the Fundamentalist Church of Jesus Christ of Latter-day Saints (FLDS) in the provision of housing, utility and policing services in violation of the Fair Housing Act (FHA). Prior to the jury verdict, the parties reached an agreement that the defendants will pay $1.6 million to resolve the monetary claim under the FHA. The jury also issued a separate advisory verdict on division's claims under Section 14141 of the Violent Crime Control and Law Enforcement Act of 1994. In its advisory verdict, the jury found that the Colorado City Marshal's Office, the cities' joint police department, operated as an arm of the FLDS church in violation of the establishment clause of the First Amendment; engaged in discriminatory policing in violation of the equal protection clause of the 14th Amendment and the establishment clause; and subjected individuals to unlawful stops, seizures and arrests in violation of the Fourth Amendment.

Scotland County, North Carolina, Public Housing Agency and Two Former Employees Agreed to Pay Over $2.7 Million to Settle Sexual Harassment Lawsuits. In July 2015, Southeastern Community and Family Services Inc. (SCFS), a public housing agency that administers the Section 8 voucher program in Scotland County, North Carolina, and two of SCFS' former employees agreed to pay more than $2.7 million in monetary damages and civil penalties to settle consolidated FHA lawsuits brought by the division and private plaintiffs. This represents the largest monetary settlement ever agreed to in a sexual harassment case brought by the Justice Department under the FHA.

Supreme Court Issued Pivotal Ruling in Fair Housing Act Case. In June 2015, in *Texas Department of Housing and Community Affairs v. Inclusive Communities Project Inc.*, the Supreme Court affirmed that the Fair Housing Act encompasses disparate impact claims, which Attorney General Lynch called "an essential tool for realizing the Act's promise of fair and open access to housing opportunities for all Americans." She added: "Bolstered by this important ruling, the Department of Justice will continue to vigorously enforce the Fair Housing Act with every tool at its disposal – including challenges based on unfair and unacceptable discriminatory effects."

Filed Brief to Address the Use of Criminal Background Checks by Housing Providers. In October 2016, the division filed a statement of interest in a New York case, *Fortune Society, Inc. v. Sandcastle Towers Housing Development Fund Corporation, et al.*, arguing that the FHA requires that landlords who consider criminal records in evaluating prospective tenants do not use overly broad generalizations that disproportionately disqualify people based on a legally protected characteristic, such as race or national origin.

UNITED STATES DISTRICT COURT
EASTERN DISTRICT OF NEW YORK

THE FORTUNE SOCIETY, INC.,	)	
Plaintiff,	)	
	)	
v.	)	Civil Action No. CV-14-6410 (VMS)
	)	
SANDCASTLE TOWERS HOUSING DEVELOPMENT FUND CORP., *et al.*,	)	
	)	
Defendants.	)	
	)	

UNITED STATES OF AMERICA'S STATEMENT OF INTEREST

DEFENDED THE RIGHTS OF SERVICEMEMBERS

No one who serves our country and puts their life on the line to protect our freedoms should ever return home to find their rights denied, their debt skyrocketing, their home foreclosed or their car repossessed. The division protects a servicemember's civilian employment rights by enforcing the Uniformed Services Employment and Reemployment Rights Act (USERRA), voting rights by enforcing the Uniformed and Overseas Citizens Absentee Voting Act of 1986 (UOCAVA) and financial security through the Servicemembers Civil Relief Act (SCRA). The Justice Department's Servicemembers and Veterans Initiative also serves as a resource for current and former members of the military and military family members, legal practitioners who serve the military community and the general public.

Settled Lawsuit Against Missouri National Guard to Enforce Employment Rights of Civilian National Guard Technician. In March 2015, the division reached a settlement with the Missouri National Guard (MNG) to resolve allegations that MNG violated USERRA by requiring its civilian National Guard dual technician employees to be separated from their civilian positions prior to entering active military duty service with the U.S. Active Guard Reserve (AGR) Program. This case represented the division's largest injunctive relief settlement in the history of its Uniformed Services Employment and Reemployment Rights Act (USERRA) enforcement program, dating back to 2004.

The division's enforcement has led to more than **140,000 service members** and their co-borrowers receiving more than **$456 million** in relief for home foreclosures, auto repossessions and interest rate overcharges.

Under the National Mortgage Settlement, Won $364 Million in Relief for 19,000 Servicemembers. Under the Servicemembers Civil Relief Act (SCRA) portions of the 2012 National Mortgage Settlement with Bank of America, Citibank, GMAC Mortgage, JP Morgan Chase and Wells Fargo, the division has directed the payment of $364 million to 19,000 servicemembers for unlawful mortgage foreclosures and mortgage interest rate overcharges.

Reached $60 Million Settlement with Sallie Mae to Resolve Allegations of Charging Military Servicemembers Excessive Rates on Student Loans. In May 2014, the division announced the federal government's first lawsuit filed against owners and servicers of student loans for violating the rights of servicemembers eligible for benefits and protections under the SCRA. The complaint alleged that three defendants, collectively known as Sallie Mae, engaged in a nationwide pattern or practice, dating as far back as 2005, of violating the SCRA by failing to provide members of the military the 6 percent interest rate cap to which they were entitled. The division then reached a settlement of the lawsuit that required Sallie Mae to pay $60 million to compensate nearly 78,000 servicemembers for the alleged SCRA violations.

Developed and Submitted Servicemembers Legislative Package to Congress. The division developed a legislative package to protect the rights of servicemembers. The proposed amendments would require parties seeking default judgments against servicemembers to first check U.S. Department of Defense records to determine duty status, making it more difficult for unscrupulous creditors to take advantage of servicemembers on active duty. The amendments also would increase penalties that employers, as well as lending and rental businesses, would face for violating laws designed to protect servicemembers. The legislative proposals expand the number and types of cases the United States could bring in defense of servicemembers attempting to return to their civilian employment upon completion of their military service and the available remedies for violations of the voting rights of servicemembers and their families while they are overseas. Additionally, the proposed amendments seek to protect military families by affording dependent family members the same state residency rights as the servicemember, as well as requiring states to recognize a servicemember spouse's professional licensures from other states. These important changes would not only enhance the Justice Department's ability to bring enforcement actions, but also enable these men and women to assert their rights on their own.

Protected the Civil Rights of LGBT Women, Men and Children

For the past eight years, the Civil Rights Division has worked tirelessly to make the promise of equal protection real for gay, lesbian, bisexual and transgender individuals. From marriage equality to protecting the civil rights of transgender women and men in education, employment and the criminal justice system, the division continues to serve as a forceful agent of justice on behalf of the LGBT community. The humiliation, frustration and embarrassment LGBT individuals feel when they are denied the equal protection of the law – when they receive the message that they are less worthy of equal status and dignity than their peers – is the pain of discrimination. And the mission of the Civil Rights Division, for decades, has always been to combat discrimination in all its forms.

Nos. 14-556, 14-562, 14-571 and 14-574

In the Supreme Court of the United States

JAMES OBERGEFELL, ET AL., PETITIONERS

v.

RICHARD HODGES, DIRECTOR, OHIO DEPARTMENT OF HEALTH, ET AL.

VALERIA TANCO, ET AL., PETITIONERS

v.

BILL HASLAM, GOVERNOR OF TENNESSEE, ET AL.

APRIL DeBOER, ET AL., PETITIONERS

v.

RICK SNYDER, GOVERNOR OF MICHIGAN, ET AL.

GREGORY BOURKE, ET AL., PETITIONERS

v.

STEVE BESHEAR, GOVERNOR OF KENTUCKY, ET AL.

---

*ON WRITS OF CERTIORARI
TO THE UNITED STATES COURT OF APPEALS
FOR THE SIXTH CIRCUIT*

**BRIEF FOR THE UNITED STATES
AS AMICUS CURIAE SUPPORTING PETITIONERS**

DONALD B. VERRILLI, JR.
*Solicitor General
Counsel of Record*

Additional Counsel Listed on Inside Cover

STATEMENT

Petitioners are same-sex couples who have been denied the privileges and responsibilities of civil marriage by the States in which they make their homes. Petitioners have formed, and seek legal recognition of, their committed relationships for the same reasons that opposite-sex couples do. But their home States persist in excluding them from the "dignity and status" of civil marriage and the "far-reaching legal acknowledgment of the intimate relationship between two people" that civil marriage represents, *United States* v. *Windsor*, 133 S. Ct. 2675, 2692 (2013). In doing so, those States have burdened petitioners in every aspect of life that marriage touches, "from the mundane to the profound," *id.* at 2694.

Defended Marriage Equality. The division worked on the Justice Department's amicus brief submitted before the U.S. Supreme Court in *Obergefell v. Hodges* – the case that held that banning same-sex couples from marrying violates the 14th Amendment. The brief recounted America's painful history of discrimination against gay and lesbian individuals and explained that such bans "exclude a long-mistreated class of human beings from a legal and social status of tremendous import" and are "incompatible with the Constitution." In June 2015, the Supreme Court agreed, ruling that the Constitution guarantees all people "equal dignity in the eyes of the law."

> "As the Constitution endures, persons in every generation can invoke its principles in their own search for greater freedom." *Lawrence*, 539 U.S. at 579. A "prime part of the history of our Constitution * * * is the story of the extension of constitutional rights and protections to people once ignored or excluded." *VMI*, 518 U.S. at 557. Here, petitioners seek the "duties and responsibilities that are an essential part of married life," *Windsor*, 133 S. Ct. at 2695, that opposite-sex couples, and tens of thousands of same-sex couples, already enjoy. The laws they challenge exclude a long-mistreated class of human beings from a legal and social status of tremendous import. Those laws are not adequately justified by any of the advanced rationales. They are accordingly incompatible with the Constitution.

Excerpts from the Justice Department's amicus brief in *Obergefell v. Hodges*.

Sued State of North Carolina to Stop Discrimination Against Transgender Individuals. In May 2016, the division filed a complaint against the state of North Carolina, the University of North Carolina (UNC) and the North Carolina Department of Public Safety (DPS) alleging that they are discriminating against transgender individuals in violation of federal law as a result of the state's compliance with and implementation of House Bill 2 (H.B. 2). H.B. 2 requires public agencies to treat transgender men, whose gender identity does not match the sex they were assigned at birth, differently from all other similarly situated men, and requires public agencies to treat transgender women differently from all other similarly situated women.

"This action is about a great deal more than just bathrooms. This is about the dignity and respect we accord our fellow citizens and the laws that we, as a people and as a country, have enacted to protect them – indeed, to protect all of us."

— Remarks of Attorney General Loretta E. Lynch at Press Conference on May 9, 2016 Announcing Complaint Against the State of North Carolina to Stop Discrimination Against Transgender Individuals

Released Guidance to Help Schools Ensure the Civil Rights of Transgender Students. The division and the U.S. Department of Education released joint guidance to provide educators the information they need to ensure that all students, including transgender students, can attend school in an environment free from discrimination based on sex. Under Title IX of the Education Amendments of 1972, schools receiving federal money may not discriminate based on a student's sex, including a student's transgender status. In plain language, the guidance offers both federal agencies' assistance to educators in their efforts to ensure that they offer a nondiscriminatory educational environment, including treating students consistent with their gender identity.

Filed Brief in Critical Transgender Rights Case Before the Fourth Circuit Court of Appeals. In October 2015, the division filed an amicus brief in the Fourth Circuit in *G.G. v. Gloucester County School Board*, a case involving a sex-discrimination claim by a transgender student under Title IX of the Education Amendments of 1972. The division's brief explained that Title IX's ban on sex discrimination prohibits schools from discriminating against students based on transgender status. The division also filed a statement of interest in the district court. In April 2016, the Fourth Circuit ruled that the district court must reevaluate a request from Gavin Grimm, a 17-year-old high school student and transgender male, to use the boys' restroom at school. The U.S. Supreme Court recently agreed to hear the case.

Filed Lawsuit Alleging that Southeastern Oklahoma State University Discriminated Against Transgender Woman. In March 2015, the division filed a lawsuit against Southeastern Oklahoma State University and the Regional University System of Oklahoma for violating Title VII of the Civil Rights Act of 1964 by discriminating against a transgender employee on the basis of her sex and retaliating against her when she complained about the discrimination. Attorney General Eric Holder announced in December 2014 that the Justice Department takes the position that Title VII's prohibition against sex discrimination is best read to include claims of discrimination based on an individual's gender identity, including transgender status.

> "Yet our journey still stretches beyond the horizon. And that's why, until we reach our destination, this Department of Justice will never back down. We will never give up. And we will never stop working to provide LGBT individuals – and all Americans – with the security and the essential protections to which they are entitled."
>
> *– Remarks from Attorney General Eric Holder at 14th Annual Lambda Legal Reception in 2014*

Fought to Protect the Rights of Transgender Prisoners in Georgia. In April 2015, the division filed a statement of interest in *Diamond v. Owens, et al.* The plaintiff in that case, a transgender prisoner, alleges that the Georgia Department of Corrections failed to provide adequate care for her gender dysphoria. The division argued that freeze-frame policies prohibiting treatment beyond the care that a prisoner received prior to incarceration violate the Eighth Amendment's ban on cruel and unusual punishment. Less than a week after the division's filing, the state abandoned its freeze-frame policy. In February 2016, the division opened a statewide investigation into the treatment of transgender and gay prisoners in the custody of the Georgia Department of Corrections. The investigation stems from allegations that state corrections officials failed to adequately investigate reports of – as well as protect transgender and gay prisoners from – rape and abuse.

FOUGHT DISCRIMINATION AND EXPANDED EQUAL OPPORTUNITY IN THE WORKPLACE

The division works to prevent workplace discrimination on the basis of race, national origin, sex, religion, disability and immigration status. It addresses discriminatory hiring practices that hold people back from pursuing their dreams and advancing their careers. It combats pregnancy and pay discrimination in the workplace: when women don't get the wages they deserve, businesses, working families and entire communities suffer. The division also combats discrimination against work-authorized immigrants and U.S. citizens, and creatively engages with the public to make sure victims know where to turn for help.

Settled Immigration-Related Discrimination Claims Against 121 Residency Programs and American Association of Colleges of Podiatric Medicine. In June 2016, the division entered into a settlement with 121 podiatry residency programs and the American Association of Colleges of Podiatric Medicine (AACPM), effectively stopping an entire industry from engaging in discriminatory job advertising. The division's investigation found that between 2013 and 2015, more than 100 podiatry residency programs and AACPM published discriminatory postings for podiatry residents through AACPM's online podiatry residency application and matching service. The division determined that hundreds of job postings limited podiatry residency positions to U.S. citizens even though there was no legal authorization for the citizenship requirement. In addition to securing over $200,000 in civil penalties, the settlement agreement required all of the programs and AACPM to change their hiring practices, policies and procedures to ensure non-discrimination.

Settled Immigration-Related Discrimination Claim Against McDonald's. In November 2015, the division entered into the second largest settlement in its 30-year history of enforcing the Immigration and Nationality Act's anti-discrimination provision, resolving claims that McDonald's USA discriminated against work-authorized immigrants. The division's investigation found that McDonald's had a longstanding practice of requiring lawful permanent residents to show a new permanent resident card when their original documents expired, even though the law prohibits this practice. The investigation also found that those lawful permanent residents who could not provide a new card upon request were not allowed to work, with some even losing their jobs as a result. The settlement required McDonald's to pay $355,000 in civil penalties, undergo monitoring and train its employees.

Settled Claim Against Nevada Taxicab Companies for Discrimination Against Immigrants. In October 2015, the division entered into a settlement that resolved claims against three taxicab companies in Las Vegas, Nevada, alleging that they required work-authorized non-U.S. citizens, but not similarly-situated U.S. citizens, to present additional and unnecessary documentation to prove their eligibility to work. Under the terms of the settlement, the taxicab companies must pay $445,000 in civil penalties, place print advertisements in a monthly trade publication advising the public of anti-discrimination law and train their employees on the relevant statute.

Settled Claims Against Barrios Street Realty Inc. for Discriminating Against U.S. Workers. In March 2016, the division reached a settlement with Barrios Street Realty Inc., which contained unprecedented relief. The agreement resolved claims that the company and a third party agent discriminated against U.S. workers by failing to consider them for positions and hiring temporary foreign workers under the H-2B visa program instead. Under the agreement, Barrios Street Realty was required to create a back pay fund of $115,000 to compensate U.S. workers and pay $30,000 in civil penalties. In addition, the company agreed to a voluntary three-year debarment from the H-2B visa program – the first time in its history that division has secured such relief.

Entered into Agreements with Foreign Governments to Improve Outreach and Protect the Rights of Immigrant Workers. Since 2015, the division has entered into four memoranda of understanding (MOUs) with foreign governments aimed at educating work-authorized immigrant workers about anti-discrimination law and creating a system of complaint referrals. Under the four MOUs – with Ecuador, El Salvador, Honduras and Mexico – the division will participate in events sponsored by the embassies and consulates aimed at educating workers about their workplace rights and train consular staff on anti-discrimination law so that they can better assist their communities. The embassies, in turn, will establish a system for referring discrimination complaints from consulates to the division. To date, the division has conducted six trainings with consular offices around the country and has received several referrals from embassies and consulates.

Issued Joint Guidance for Employers Conducting Internal Employment Eligibility Verification Form I-9 Audits. In December 2015, the division and U.S. Immigration and Customs Enforcement (ICE) jointly published, "Guidance for Employers Conducting Internal Employment Eligibility Verification Form I-9 Audits," the first time the division has issued guidance jointly with ICE. The guidance provides employers with information regarding how to conduct a review of their Forms I-9 without violating the anti-discrimination provision of the Immigration and Naturalization Act or Form I-9 rules. Since its publication, the guidance has been praised by employee and employer groups.

Supervised Payment of Nearly $100 Million to Victims of Discriminatory Hiring by the New York Fire Department. In 2015, through the enforcement of Title VII, and under the supervision of the division, the city of New York paid approximately $99 million dollars to victims of discriminatory hiring policies that occurred in the New York Fire Department (FDNY). The sums obtained consist of compensation for the persons harmed by the city's discriminatory testing policies in the form of back-pay, lost fringe benefits and interest, and are the largest damages ever obtained by the division in an employment case. More than six years after the court found the city liable under Title VII and following five years of hard-fought remedial phase litigation, more than 1,400 African-American and Hispanic applicants harmed by the city's use of unlawful entrance exams were compensated for back pay, lost fringe benefits and interest.

Settled Employment Discrimination Lawsuit Against Lubbock, Texas. The division brought groundbreaking litigation under Title VII against the city of Lubbock, Texas, Police Department by, for the first time, seeking and obtaining relief in a single lawsuit for two different protected classes, Hispanics and women, impacted by two separate selection devices. Under the terms of a court-ordered consent decree, the city will pay a total of $725,000 in back pay to victims of the discriminatory employment tests; develop a new written test and a new physical fitness test for hiring probationary police officers; and provide hiring relief, including retroactive seniority, to 11 qualified Hispanic and 13 female applicants who were disqualified by the challenged employment tests.

Settled Employment Discrimination Lawsuit Against City of Chicago Police Department. In February 2016, the division announced a settlement of its employment lawsuit against the city of Chicago Police Department by which the city agreed to pay more than $2 million as back pay to applicants born outside the United States who were disqualified from the entry-level police officer hiring process due to the unnecessarily lengthy residency requirement successfully challenged by the United States. Through the division's lawsuit, it obtained eight jobs for those otherwise qualified applicants who were harmed by the city's discriminatory practices and mandated required changes to the city's hiring and training practices as well as other favorable injunctive relief.

Released Comprehensive Report on Advancing Diversity in Law Enforcement. The Justice Department and the Equal Employment Opportunity Commission (EEOC) released a comprehensive report that examines barriers and promising practices – in recruitment, hiring and retention – for advancing diversity in law enforcement. The report, developed with support from the Center for Policing Equity, aims to provide law enforcement agencies, especially small and mid-size agencies, with a resource to enhance the diversity of their workforce by highlighting specific strategies and efforts in place in police departments around the country. The report, which builds on the recommendations of the President's Task Force on 21st Century Policing, notes that while greater workforce diversity alone cannot ensure fair and effective policing, a significant – and growing – body of evidence suggests that diversity can make policing more effective, more safe and more just. The division also partnered with U.S. Attorneys around the country to host a series of "Diversity Dialogues" in Savannah, Georgia; Wichita, Kansas; and Madison, Wisconsin, to help local law enforcement leaders share and implement some of the promising practices identified in the report.

Settled Pregnancy and Disability Discrimination Lawsuit Against City of Florence, Kentucky. The division reinforced, as a strategic priority, Title VII's mandate against discrimination against pregnant women by investigating, filing suit and settling the Justice Department's first case enforcing the Pregnancy Discrimination Act (PDA) after the Supreme Court's decision in *Young v. UPS*. The Florence, Kentucky, Police Department had a policy that allowed workers to take light duty when necessary. After a female police officer took light duty while pregnant pursuant this policy, Florence changed its policy to one that was much more restrictive – and which discriminated against pregnant employees. During the division's investigation, the *Young* decision set out a method of proving that restrictions on light duty could be violations of the PDA, something that most circuits had rejected before that point. The consent decree with Florence provides for new policies and compensatory damages for the pregnant women who were denied light duty under Florence's restrictive policies.

> **"No woman should ever have to choose between having a family and earning a salary."**
>
> *— Head of the Civil Rights Division Vanita Gupta*

Sued South Dakota State Agency for Discrimination Against Native American Job Applicants at Pine Ridge Reservation. In 2015, the division sued the South Dakota Department of Social Services (DSS), alleging that DSS discriminated against an aggrieved Native-American applicant for employment and other similarly situated individuals, and engaged in a pattern or practice of discrimination against Native Americans, when it failed to select Native American applicants for a series of positions in DSS's office located on the Pine Ridge Indian Reservation. This type of discrimination is devastating to Native-American populations already facing limited employment opportunities and was exacerbated by the employer's ever-shifting and discredited explanations for the discrimination. The lawsuit constitutes the division's first employment case brought on behalf of Native Americans in more than 10 years.

Sued New Mexico State University Alleging Discrimination in Pay Against Female Coach. In August 2016, the division filed a lawsuit alleging that New Mexico State University and its Board of Regents discriminated against a female former assistant track coach on the basis of sex by paying her less than similarly-situated men in violation of Title VII of the Civil Rights Act of 1964.

Filed Lawsuit Alleging Sex Discrimination Against the Commonwealth of Pennsylvania and the Pennsylvania State Police. In July 2014, the division filed a lawsuit against the Commonwealth of Pennsylvania and the Pennsylvania State Police, alleging that the defendants are engaged in a pattern or practice of employment discrimination against women in violation of Title VII of the Civil Rights Act of 1964. Specifically, the lawsuit challenges the state police's use of two physical fitness tests to screen and select entry-level state troopers. It alleges that the physical fitness tests used by the state police between 2003 and the present excluded qualified women from consideration for hire as entry-level state troopers by testing for physical skills that are not actually required to perform the job. It also alleges that, during the relevant time period, the defendants' use of physical fitness tests as part of a multi-step employment selection process disproportionately screened out female applicants, resulting in a disparate impact against those applicants.

ADVANCED CONSTITUTIONAL POLICING

The vast majority of men and women who wear the badge serve our communities with professionalism, integrity and distinction. Yet when police departments engage in a pattern or practice of unconstitutional policing, their actions can severely erode community trust and profoundly undermine public safety. More than two decades ago, Congress charged the Justice Department with the responsibility of enforcing Section 14141 of the Violent Crime Control and Law Enforcement Act of 1994. This statute authorizes the division to investigate local law enforcement agencies for a pattern or practice of misconduct that violates federal law and, where necessary, to file litigation to ensure reform. During this administration, the division has opened 25 civil pattern-or-practice investigations into local law enforcement agencies to investigate allegations of misconduct, including excessive force; unlawful stops, searches and arrests; and discriminatory policing, among others. If the division identifies a pattern or practice of unlawful conduct, it tries to negotiate a settlement agreement with the jurisdiction, most often in the form of a court-approved, independently-monitored consent decree.

Opened Pattern-or-Practice Investigation into the Chicago Police Department. In December 2015, the division opened a civil pattern-or-practice investigation into the Chicago Police Department (CPD), pursuant to the Violent Crime Control and Law Enforcement Act of 1994. The department's investigation of CPD seeks to determine whether there are systemic violations of the Constitution or federal law by officers of CPD. The investigation is focused on CPD's use of force, including racial, ethnic and other disparities in use of force, and its systems of accountability.

Announced Findings of Investigation into Baltimore City Police Department. In August 2016, the division announced that it found reasonable cause to believe that the Baltimore City Police Department (BPD) engages in a pattern or practice of conduct that violates the First and Fourth Amendments of the Constitution as well as federal anti-discrimination laws. BPD makes stops, searches and arrests without the required justification; uses enforcement strategies that unlawfully subject African Americans to disproportionate rates of stops, searches and arrests; uses excessive force; and retaliates against individuals for their constitutionally-protected expression. The pattern or practice results from systemic deficiencies that have persisted within BPD for many years and has exacerbated community distrust of the police, particularly in the African-American community. The city and the division have also entered into an agreement in principle to work together, with community input, to create a federal court-enforceable consent decree addressing the deficiencies found during the investigation.

Released Report on Division's Pattern and Practice Police Reform Work. In January 2017, the division released a comprehensive report that provides an overview of its police reform work under Section 14141. The report is designed to serve as a resource for local law enforcement agencies and communities by making the division's police reform work more accessible and transparent.

Resolved Lawsuit Against City of Ferguson, Missouri, with Agreement to Reform Ferguson Police Department and Municipal Court to Ensure Constitutional Policing. In March 2016, the division and the city of Ferguson, Missouri, announced an agreement resolving the division's pending lawsuit against Ferguson. The court-enforceable decree aims to remedy the unconstitutional law enforcement conduct that the Justice Department found during its civil pattern-or-practice investigation into the Ferguson Police Department (FPD) and the Ferguson Municipal Court. The findings from the division's investigation, which were announced in March 2015, launched a national conversation about the connections among policing, poverty, race and injustice. In addition to discriminatory policing against African-American residents, the division found that the city was using policing as a means to generate revenue, imposing excessive fines and fees against residents that resulted, in effect, in the criminalization of poverty. As of August 2016, the consent decree resulted in dismissal of more than 32,000 unwarranted court cases and cancellation of more than $1.5 million in fines.

Municipal Court Practices

Ferguson has allowed its focus on revenue generation to fundamentally compromise the role of Ferguson's municipal court. The municipal court does not act as a neutral arbiter of the law or a check on unlawful police conduct. Instead, the court primarily uses its judicial authority as the means to compel the payment of fines and fees that advance the City's financial interests. This has led to court practices that violate the Fourteenth Amendment's due process and equal protection requirements. The court's practices also impose unnecessary harm, overwhelmingly on African-American individuals, and run counter to public safety.

Excerpt of the Civil Rights Division's Findings Letter from its Investigation into the Ferguson Police Department and Municipal Court.

"Our Ferguson report resonated so widely because it gave voice to the sometimes subtle, but dangerous ways that the justice system can corrode a community's belief that its government operates fairly. The belief – so essential to effective self-governance and the rule of law – that public institutions treat people with dignity and decency."

– Head of the Civil Rights Division Vanita Gupta

Reached Agreement with City of Seattle to Implement Reforms of Seattle Police Department. In July 2012, the division entered into a comprehensive agreement with the city of Seattle to implement sustainable reforms within the Seattle Police Department (SPD). The agreement requires SPD to revise its use of force policies and enhance its training, reporting, investigations and supervision of uses of force. It also requires revisions to policies, training and supervision relating to both bias-free policing and stops and detentions; improves supervision and accountability mechanisms to ensure implementation of the reforms on the ground; and creates the Community Police Commission, a civilian oversight board with responsibilities regarding particular areas of reform detailed in the settlement agreement. A recent survey commissioned by the federal monitor and released in October 2016 found that the number of people who approve of SPD has increased to 72 percent, up from 60 percent in 2013 and 64 percent in 2015. Much of that improvement is among African Americans (49 percent approval in 2013 to 62 percent now) and Latinos (54 percent in 2013 to 74 percent now).

Reached Settlement with City of New Orleans to Resolve Allegations of Unlawful Misconduct by New Orleans Police Department. The division entered into a comprehensive, cooperative consent decree with the city of New Orleans, which was approved by the court in January 2013, to resolve allegations of unlawful police misconduct by the New Orleans Police Department (NOPD). The consent decree requires NOPD to make broad changes in policies and practices related to use of force; stops, searches and arrests; custodial interrogations; photographic line-ups; preventing discriminatory policing; community engagement; recruitment; training; officer assistance and support; performance evaluations and promotions; supervision; misconduct investigations; and NOPD's system of secondary employment, also known as paid details.

Reached Police Reform Agreement with Portland, Oregon. In August 2014, a federal court approved a comprehensive settlement agreement that the division reached with the Portland Oregon Police Bureau (PPB) to reform how PBB interacts with individuals with actual or perceived mental illness. The agreement requires changes – many of which PPB has already begun to implement – in policies, training, supervisory oversight, community-based mental health services, crisis intervention, employee information systems, officer accountability and community engagement and oversight. The agreement also calls for innovative new mechanisms for ongoing community involvement in the implementation of reforms.

Reached Agreement with City of Cleveland to Reform Cleveland Division of Police Following the Finding of a Pattern or Practice of Excessive Force. In May 2015, the division reached a comprehensive court-enforceable agreement with the city of Cleveland to address the division's findings that the Cleveland Division of Police (CDP) engages in a pattern or practice of using excessive force in violation of the Fourth Amendment. The agreement creates widespread reforms and changes within the CDP. The changes focus on building community trust; reforming stop, search and arrest practices; creating a culture of community and problem-oriented policing; officer safety and training; officer accountability; and technological upgrades.

Reached Agreement with City of Newark, New Jersey, to Reform Police Department's Unconstitutional Practices. In March 2016, the division reached a comprehensive settlement with the city of Newark, New Jersey, that will bring wide-ranging reforms and changes to the Newark Police Department (NPD). The agreement resolves the department's findings that NPD has engaged in a pattern or practice of unconstitutional stops, searches, arrests, use of excessive force and theft by officers in violation of the First, Fourth and 14th Amendments. The consent decree also resolves the division's findings that NPD's law enforcement practices had a disparate impact on minorities in Newark.

Los Angeles County Sheriff's Department Agreed to Policing Reforms and Settlement of Police-Related Fair Housing Claims in the Antelope Valley. In April 2015, the division reached a comprehensive, court-enforceable settlement agreement with the Los Angeles County Sheriff's Department (LASD) that will support wide-ranging reforms in LASD's Antelope Valley stations in the cities of Lancaster and Palmdale. The agreement requires reforms to LASD's data collection, training and accountability systems to improve the quality and effectiveness of LASD's interactions with Antelope Valley residents and reduce bias in its practices. The settlement agreement also provides for a monetary fund of $700,000 to compensate persons harmed by LASD's alleged violation of the Fair Housing Act and a civil penalty of $25,000 to the United States.

Missoula Police Department Fully Implemented Agreement to Improve Response to Reports of Sexual Assault. In May 2015, the division announced that that the Missoula, Montana, Police Department (MPD) had fully implemented the requirements of its agreement with the division to improve MPD's response to reports of sexual assault. The agreement, which was entered into in May 2013, resolved part of the department's comprehensive investigation of the response by the Missoula criminal justice system and the University of Montana to sexual assault. MPD's implementation of the agreement has resulted in a host of historic advances in the Missoula response to sexual assault.

Opened Investigations of Orange County, California, District Attorney's Office and Sheriff's Department. In December 2016, the division opened a civil pattern-or-practice investigation into the Orange County District Attorney's Office and the Orange County Sheriff's Department, pursuant to the Violent Crime Control and Law Enforcement Act of 1994. The investigation will focus on allegations that the district attorney's office and the sheriff's department systematically used jailhouse informants to elicit incriminating statements from specific inmates who had been charged and were represented by counsel, in violation of the Sixth Amendment. Additionally, the investigation will seek to determine whether the district attorney's office committed systematic violations of defendants' 14th Amendment due process rights under *Brady v. Maryland*, a 1963 Supreme Court case, by failing to disclose promises of leniency that would have substantially undermined the credibility of the informants' trial testimony.

Issued Guidance on Identifying and Preventing Gender Bias in Law Enforcement Response to Sexual Assault and Domestic Violence. The division worked on Justice Department guidance, released in December 2015, which is designed to help law enforcement agencies prevent gender bias in their response to sexual assault and domestic violence. The guidance highlights the need for clear policies, robust training and responsive accountability systems. It aims to examine how gender bias can undermine the response of law enforcement agencies to sexual assault and domestic violence. It also provides a set of basic principles that – if integrated into agencies' policies, trainings and practices – will help ensure that gender bias, either intentionally or unintentionally, does not undermine efforts to keep victims safe and hold offenders accountable.

Clarified that the ADA Applies to Arrests of Individuals with Disabilities. In June 2016, the division filed a statement of interest in *Robinson v. Farley*, a case in which the plaintiff alleged that officers of the District of Columbia violated Title II of the ADA when they failed to reasonably accommodate his disabilities during his arrest and post-arrest proceedings. The division filed the statement of interest to clarify that Title II of the ADA applied to the arrest of an individual with a disability and to explain the application of Title II's reasonable modification requirement in that context.

Filed Briefs to Protect First Amendment Right to Record Police Activity. Building on its enforcement work and reforms developed in its consent decrees, the division filed multiple briefs to protect individuals' First Amendment right to record police activity. In January 2012, the division filed a statement of interest in *Sharp v. Baltimore City Police Department, et al.*, arguing that individuals have a First Amendment right to record police officers in the public discharge of their duties and officers violate individuals' Fourth and 14th Amendment rights when they seize and destroy such recordings without a warrant or due process. In March 2013, the division filed a statement of interest in *Garcia v. Montgomery County, et al.*, arguing that courts should closely scrutinize discretionary charges, such as disorderly conduct, when they arise out of an individual's attempt to record or observe police conduct. In October 2016, the division filed an amicus brief in the U.S. Court of Appeals for the Third Circuit in *Geraci and Fields v. City of Philadelphia, et al.* arguing that individuals have a First Amendment right to record police activity in public without having to challenge or criticize police officers' conduct.

PROSECUTED CRIMINAL LAW ENFORCEMENT MISCONDUCT

For decades, under two federal statutes known as Section 241 and Section 242, the division has conducted thorough, impartial investigations of individual officers for criminal violations of constitutional rights. This means pursuing criminal charges when the evidence supports them; from 2009 – 2016, the division has charged more than 580 law enforcement officials for committing willful violations of civil rights and related crimes. But it also means closing cases when the evidence does not support charges. In use-of-force cases that the division brings, federal law requires the government to prove both that the officer used "objectively unreasonable" force and that he or she acted willfully – "for the specific purpose of violating the law" – one of the highest standards of criminal intent.

Convicted 16 Correctional Officers for Abusing Inmate at Roxbury, Maryland, Correctional Institution. The division convicted 16 Maryland corrections officials for abusing an inmate at the Roxbury Correctional Institution. After the inmate assaulted an officer, multiple officers from that shift abused the inmate in retaliation. Many hours later, a new group of officers from the next shift also beat the inmate in retaliation for his prior misconduct. The next day, officers from a third shift again abused the inmate in order to continue the retaliation.

Convicted Multiple Officers for their Roles in Fatal Beating of Inmate at Alabama Correctional Facility. The division convicted multiple officers for their roles in the fatal beating of an inmate at the Ventress Correctional Facility in Clayton, Alabama, in August 2010, and the subsequent coverup. The victim was assaulted first in an office in the prison, where he was repeatedly struck with a baton, stomped and kicked. The victim was assaulted again several minutes later in the medical unit where a defendant repeatedly stomped on the victim's head.

> From 2009 – 2016, the division has **charged more than 580 law enforcement officials** for committing willful violations of civil rights and related crimes.

Convicted Two New Orleans Police Officers on Civil Rights and Obstruction of Justice Charges in Connection with the Beating Death of a Civilian. The division prosecuted two New Orleans Police Department officers (who were sentenced in September 2011) in connection with the death of Raymond Robair in New Orleans. When the officers, in their patrol car, approached Robair on the street, Robair ran and the officers chased him. One of the officers caught Robair and beat him viciously with a baton. Both officers then dragged Robair into their car, drove him to the hospital, and dropped him off in the emergency room, telling medical staff that they had "found him beneath a bridge." Because they were unaware that Robair was suffering from blunt force trauma, medical authorities were unable to treat him effectively. Robair died from his injuries. At trial, the jury convicted Officer Williams of violating Robair's civil rights and convicted both officers of obstruction.

Charged Former North Charleston, South Carolina, Police Officer Michael Slager with Federal Civil Rights Offense. In May 2016, a federal grand jury returned a three-count indictment charging former North Charleston, South Carolina, Police Department (NCPD) Officer Michael Slager with federal offenses related to his fatal shooting of Walter Scott on April 4, 2015. The indictment includes charges for a federal civil rights offense, using a firearm during the commission of the civil rights offense and obstruction of justice. The indictment alleges that Michael Slager, while acting as an NCPD Officer, used excessive force when he shot and killed Walter Scott without legal justification.

PROSECUTED HUMAN TRAFFICKING

The division works to combat the scourge of human trafficking – a form of modern-day slavery in which victims are exploited for forced labor or commercial sex, often enduring sexual assault, brutality, psychological coercion, threats and fear. Traffickers may act alone or through international organized criminal networks, and victims include both U.S. citizens and foreign nationals. Prosecuting these cases presents unique challenges, as each requires a dedication of time, resources and specialized skill in jurisdictions across the country and around the globe.

Prosecuted Record Numbers of Human Trafficking Cases. From 2009 – 2016, the division, in partnership with United States Attorneys' Offices, initiated 521 human trafficking cases, charged 1,182 defendants, and convicted 782 defendants in cases involving forced labor and adult and international sex trafficking. These numbers reflect increases of over 165 percent in cases filed, over 122 percent in defendants charged and over 86 percent in defendants convicted, compared to the prior eight-year period (2001 – 2008).

Launched the Interagency Anti-Trafficking Coordination Team (ACTeam) Initiative. In December 2015, the Departments of Justice, Homeland Security and Labor announced the designation of six Phase II Anti-Trafficking Coordination Teams (ACTeams) identified through a competitive, nationwide, interagency selection process. The launch of Phase II built on the momentum generated in Phase I of the ACTeam Initiative, in which Phase I Pilot ACTeams convened in 2012-2013 significantly increased human trafficking prosecutions. The interagency ACTeam Initiative, led by the division's Human Trafficking Prosecution Unit, brings together specialized teams of federal agents and federal prosecutors to implement coordinated, interagency strategic action plans to combat identified human trafficking threats involving forced labor, international sex trafficking and sex trafficking of adults, in collaboration with national anti-trafficking subject matter experts from the Departments of Justice, Homeland Security and Labor.

Led the U.S.-Mexico Bilateral Human Trafficking Enforcement Initiative. Since 2009, the division's Human Trafficking Prosecution Unit has collaborated with the Department of Homeland Security and Mexican law enforcement counterparts to lead a Bilateral Human Trafficking Enforcement Initiative aimed at strengthening high-impact prosecutions under both U.S. and Mexican law. These efforts have resulted in successful prosecutions in both Mexico and the United States, including U.S. federal prosecutions of over 50 defendants in multiple cases in New York, Georgia, Florida and Texas; numerous Mexican federal and state prosecutions of associated sex traffickers; and coordinated, bilateral enforcement actions to dismantle notorious transnational sex trafficking enterprises.

Convicted Florida Man of Sex Trafficking in Connection with Human Trafficking Scheme Targeting Foreign University Students. In November 2016, a Florida man was convicted on all 11 counts for organizing a scheme to lure foreign university students into the United States under false pretenses of legitimate summer jobs, only to advertise the students to customers of his prostitution and erotic massage enterprise. He was convicted of sex trafficking and attempted sex trafficking by fraud, wire fraud, importation of persons for prostitution or immoral purposes and use of a facility of interstate commerce to operate a prostitution enterprise. A jury in the Southern District of Florida returned the verdict after four days of trial.

Heroin Dealer Convicted by Jury of Sex Trafficking and Drug-Related Offenses. In July 2016, a Wisconsin man was convicted by a federal jury of three counts of sex trafficking by force, threats of force or coercion; one count of conspiracy to engage in interstate transportation for prostitution; one count of interstate transportation for prostitution; one count of maintaining a property for drug trafficking; one count of using a firearm in furtherance of drug trafficking and one count of witness retaliation. The defendant sold heroin and used violence, threats and coercion to compel three young heroin-addicted women to prostitute for his profit in Wisconsin and Minnesota.

Defendants Charged in Connection with Mexican Sex Trafficking Enterprise Extradited to U.S. In November 2015, U.S. and Mexican authorities conducted a coordinated, bilateral law enforcement operation to simultaneously apprehend defendants in both Mexico and the U.S. and secure the June 2016 extradition of five defendants from Mexico to the U.S. on charges of operating an organized sex trafficking enterprise that used deception, psychological coercion, threats and violence to compel young, vulnerable women and girls into prostitution. Eight defendants were charged with sex trafficking and related offenses in a 27-count indictment returned in the Eastern District of New York.

Lead Defendant Sentenced to Over 15 years for Labor Trafficking of Vulnerable Guatemalan Migrants. In June 2016, the leader of a human trafficking organization was sentenced to over 15 years in prison and ordered to pay over $67,000 in restitution to the victims of a forced labor scheme that targeted Guatemalan migrants, including both adults and minors as young as 14 or 15. Six defendants were convicted in connection with the case for their respective roles in luring the victims to the United States under false pretenses, then using threats of physical harm to compel them to perform physically demanding work at an Ohio egg farm for over 12 hours a day, with minimal pay.

PROSECUTED HATE CRIMES

The division prosecutes hate crimes, which include acts of physical harm and specific criminal threats motivated by animus based on race, color, national origin, religion, gender, sexual orientation, gender identity or disability. Hate crimes have a devastating effect beyond the harm inflicted on any one victim. They reverberate through families, communities and the entire nation, as others fear that they too could be threatened, attacked or forced from their homes because of what they look like, who they are, where they worship, whom they love or whether they have a disability.

Prosecuted First Case Under Matthew Shepard and James Byrd Jr. Hate Crimes Prevention Act Where Victim was Targeted Because of Gender Identity. In December 2016, Joshua Brandon Vallum, 29, of Lucedale, Mississippi, pleaded guilty to a federal hate crime for assaulting and murdering Mercedes Williamson because she was a transgender woman. Williamson was 17 years old and resided in Alabama at the time of her death. Vallum was charged with violating the Matthew Shepard and James Byrd Jr. Hate Crimes Prevention Act. In a statement, Attorney General Lynch said: "Our nation's hate crime statutes advance one of our fundamental beliefs: that no one should have to live in fear because of who they are. Today's landmark guilty plea reaffirms that basic principle, and it signals the Justice Department's determination to combat hate crimes based on gender identity."

Convicted Defendant for Setting Fire to Missouri Mosque. In April 2016, a man pleaded guilty to a federal hate crime for setting a fire that destroyed the Islamic Society of Joplin mosque. The defendant admitted that he set fire to the mosque because he does not like the Islamic religion. As a direct result of the fire, many donations made during the Muslim holy period of Ramadan were destroyed.

Convicted Two Men for Vicious Assault on Gay African-American Man. In February 2016, two men were each sentenced to 15 years in prison following their convictions of hate crime offenses for their roles in a March 2012 assault of a gay African-American man in Corpus Christi, Texas. The two men admitted they conspired to assault the victim because of his race and sexual orientation. They admitted to punching and kicking the man and assaulting him with various weapons including a frying pan, a mug, a sock filled with batteries, a broom and a belt. During the course of the assault, the victim was forced to remove his clothing and clean up his own blood. When the victim was completely naked, one of the defendants held a gun to the victim's head, while another defendant sodomized the victim with a broom handle. In addition, one of the defendants poured bleach onto the victim's face and eyes, and struck him with a handgun. The defendants also whipped the victim on the back with a belt. During the assault, the defendants repeatedly used both racial and homophobic slurs.

Convicted 10 Defendants for their Roles in Racially-Motivated Assault and Murder of African-American Man. Ten people in Mississippi pleaded guilty for their roles in the racially-motivated assault and murder of an African-American man in June 2011 or to related charges of conspiring to assault and harass African-American residents of Jackson, Mississippi by (among other things) hurling beer bottles at them and by beating them and kicking them with steel-toe boots. The defendants have been sentenced to federal prison terms ranging from four to 50 years. The 50-year term went to Deryl Paul Dedmon, the pickup truck driver who ran over the victim. Dedmon was also charged in state court with murder and received two life sentences.

> ## "Today we take another step away from Mississippi's tortured past ... we move farther away from the abyss."
>
> *— Remarks from U.S. District Judge Carlton Reeves of the Southern District of Mississippi at a 2015 Sentencing Hearing*

Organized Regional Trainings for State and Local Law Enforcement. In partnership with U.S. Attorneys, in 2015 the division helped organized a series of regional trainings – in Mississippi, California, Oregon, Kansas and Florida – to train local and federal law enforcement in how to recognize, investigate and prove hate crimes; to educate communities and engage them in the process of ensuring public safety; and to encourage better hate crime reporting and data collection.

Protected Access to Reproductive Health Care

The division enforces the Freedom of Access to Clinic Entrances (FACE) Act, which protects the exercise of free choice in obtaining reproductive health services and the exercise of First Amendment religious freedoms. While people have a First Amendment right to peacefully express their views, they do not have a right to vandalize clinics in the hopes of deterring women from receiving lawful services that those facilities provide.

Baltimore Man Convicted for Damaging Property of a Reproductive Health Services Facility. In October 2016, a Baltimore man pleaded guilty to one count of violating the Freedom of Access to Clinic Entrances (FACE) Act, which makes it a federal crime to damage the property of a reproductive health services facility because of the services offered there. The charge stems from incidents that occurred in February 2016, when the defendant, Travis Reynolds, and another man decided to vandalize a Baltimore area women's health care clinic. Reynolds spray-painted the words "Baby Killer," "Kill Baby Here" and other graphic messages across the building where the clinic is located. At the time of his arrest, Reynolds admitted to police that he defaced the clinic's doors, walls and windows because he thought that it would deter women from using the clinic.

Missouri Man Convicted for Arson at Mosque and Attempted Arson at Planned Parenthood. In April 2016, a Missouri man pleaded guilty to two attempts to set fire to the Planned Parenthood facility in Joplin. In both instances, he threw items containing an accelerant onto the roof of the facility and then ignited material attached to the accelerant. He was apprehended soon after the Planned Parenthood arson attempts. He admitted to investigators that he was responsible for both Planned Parenthood arson attempts and that he targeted Planned Parenthood because they provide reproductive health care services.

DEFENDED THE BEDROCK OF OUR DEMOCRACY – THE RIGHT TO VOTE

The integrity of our democracy depends on ensuring that every eligible voter can meaningfully participate in the electoral process. Voting forms the bedrock of our democracy. The division works to ensure that every eligible voter enjoys the full range of voting rights protected by federal law. Even with the severe setback of the Supreme Court's 2013 decision in *Shelby County v. Holder*, the division has continued to use every tool at its disposal, including the Voting Rights Act, to protect voters from discrimination and provide the opportunities federal law guarantees.

Won Voting Rights Act Case in North Carolina to Prevent Intentional Statewide Discrimination. In the immediate aftermath of *Shelby County v. Holder*, when North Carolina passed an omnibus voting law designed to impede the ways that newly engaged minority citizens participated in the voting process, the division filed suit. In July 2016, the U.S. Court of Appeals for the Fourth Circuit struck down a North Carolina law that the court described in its ruling as "one of the largest restrictions of the franchise in modern North Carolina history" with provisions that "target African Americans with almost surgical precision."

Won Voting Rights Act Case in Texas After Years of Litigation Prolonged by *Shelby County v. Holder*. Also in July 2016, the full U.S. Court of Appeals for the Fifth Circuit held that Texas's 2011 photographic voter identification law violates Section 2 of the Voting Rights Act. This decision affirmed the Justice Department's position that Texas's highly restrictive voter ID law abridges the right to vote on account of race or color, and ordered appropriate relief. Both the North Carolina and Texas cases were among the most complex and resource-intensive cases ever brought under Section 2 of the Voting Rights Act.

Reached Major National Voter Registration Act Settlements with Alabama and Connecticut. The division entered into two major settlements under the National Voter Registration Act (NVRA). In November 2015, the division reached a comprehensive settlement with the state of Alabama over enforcement of Section 5 of the NVRA in connection with driver license transactions, and reached a similar settlement with the state of Connecticut in August 2016. These settlements require the states to ensure that voter registration opportunities are provided to citizens applying for or renewing their driver licenses, and updating their addresses for driver license purposes, whether in person or remotely, in the manner required by the NVRA.

Brought Litigation and Reached Agreements to Protect Rights of Military and Overseas Voters. In 2009 Congress enacted the Military and Overseas Voter Empowerment Act (MOVE Act), which made broad amendments to the Uniformed and Overseas Citizens Absentee Voting Act (UOCAVA). Among the new protections was a requirement that states transmit absentee ballots to voters covered under UOCAVA, by mail or electronically at the voter's option, no later than 45 days before federal elections. Since the law's 2010 effective date, the division has obtained numerous court orders or agreements to obtain compliance with the Act throughout the country and help ensure that military servicemembers, their families and U.S. citizens living overseas have the opportunity to participate in all federal elections. For example, for the 2010 federal general election, the division obtained court orders, court-approved consent decrees or out-of-court letter or memorandum agreements in 11 states, two territories and the District of Columbia. In subsequent cases, the division obtained favorable judgments in cases against New York to require an earlier federal primary election date to ensure timely ballot transmission and against Alabama and Georgia to ensure compliance with UOCAVA in federal run-off elections. It entered consent decrees with Illinois to obtain compliance in special elections to fill congressional vacancies and obtained court-ordered relief to ensure military and overseas voters in West Virginia could have their ballots counted in the 2014 federal general election. The division also proposed additional legislation to further protect the voting rights of military and overseas voters.

Sought to Expand Access to the Ballot Box for American Indians and Alaska Natives. The division worked on the Justice Department's proposed legislation – announced in May 2015 – that would require states or localities whose territory includes part or all of an Indian reservation, an Alaska Native village or other tribal lands to locate at least one polling place in a venue selected by the tribal government. American Indians and Alaska Natives have faced significant obstacles that have prevented them from enjoying equal access to polling places and equal opportunities to cast a ballot. In addition to suffering from a long history of discrimination, the distance many American Indian and Alaska Native citizens must travel to reach a polling place presents a substantial and ongoing barrier to full voter participation. This legislation would significantly mitigate that burden.

Conducted Robust Election Monitoring Program to Enforce Federal Voting Rights Laws. The division continued evaluating and monitoring all types of elections around the country on the ground on election days occurring all throughout each year, even after the Supreme Court's decision in *Shelby County v. Holder* limited the division's capacity. For example, in the November 2016 general election, the division coordinated the deployment of more than 500 personnel to monitor elections in 67 jurisdictions in 28 states for compliance with the federal voting rights laws.

Launched ADA Voting Initiative. In 2015, the division, partnering with U.S. Attorneys across the nation, launched the ADA Voting Initiative to ensure that people with disabilities have an equal opportunity to participate in the voting process, including in the 2016 presidential elections. The ADA Voting Initiative covers all aspects of voting, from voter registration to casting ballots at neighborhood polling places. Through this initiative, more than 1,300 polling places have been surveyed to identify barriers to access.

Reached Settlement with Augusta County, Virginia, Regarding Polling Place Accessibility Under the ADA. In November 2015, the division reached a settlement agreement with Augusta County, Virginia, resolving claims that the county violated the ADA by discriminating against voters with disabilities when it failed to provide accessible polling places. Many polling places in Augusta County had architectural barriers that made them inaccessible to voters who use wheelchairs or have mobility or vision impairments.

Won Voter Intimidation Conviction. In 2014, in *United States v. Baker*, the division obtained its first ever conviction under 18 U.S.C. § 594 – a voter intimidation statue. Prior to the 2012 federal elections, the defendant created and sent 200 fake voter eligibility letters to Republican Party donors across Florida that questioned the recipients' citizenship status. During the plea hearing, the defendant admitted that he intended the letters to look as if they were written by county elections officials and that his purpose in sending the letters was to intimidate the recipients and interfere with their right to vote.

Filed Dozens of Briefs to Inform Courts in Protecting the Franchise. The division filed or contributed to numerous statements of interest or amicus briefs during the administration, 16 of them in 2015 and 2016. These briefs have been filed in the Supreme Court, the courts of appeals, and the district courts around the country. This has included amicus participation in 10 cases in the Supreme Court that implicated the voting rights statutes enforced by the division, such as *McCrory v. Harris, Bethune-Hill v. Virginia State Board of Elections, Wittman v. Personhuballah, Harris v. Arizona Independent Redistricting Commission, Evenwel v. Abbott, Arizona State Legislature v. Arizona Redistricting Commission, Alabama Legislative Black Caucus v. Alabama, Alabama Democratic Conference v. Alabama, Arizona v. The Inter Tribal Council of Arizona, Perry v. Perez and Simmons v. Galvin.*

Reached Agreement to Protect the Rights of Spanish-Speaking Voters in Napa County, California. In June 2016, the division reached an agreement with Napa County, California, to ensure compliance with provisions of the Voting Rights Act that required the county to provide bilingual election materials and information in Spanish to voters. The Voting Rights Act requires that jurisdictions determined by the Census Bureau to have a substantial population of minority-language citizens with limited English proficiency, like Napa County through 2016, provide voting materials and assistance in the minority language as well as in English. The division has reached similar types of agreements with other jurisdictions in recent years to protect the rights of LEP voters, including Orange County, New York; Colfax County, Nebraska; Cuyahoga and Lorain Counties, Ohio; and Alameda and Riverside Counties, California.

PROMOTED ACCESS TO JUSTICE

Throughout the justice system – from arraignment to sentencing – when people experience a two-tiered system of justice that stacks the deck against those living in poverty, these practices erode trust in public institutions. The division, along with the department's Office for Access to Justice, has helped lead the charge against criminal justice policies that punish poverty. When people are punished for their poverty, it creates a cycle of disastrous consequences: they may lose their jobs, their health benefits or their homes without any benefit to public safety. Preventing the punishment of poverty and ensuring access to justice for all is critical to restoring and maintaining the public's faith in the legitimacy of our institutions and the integrity of our democracy.

Challenged the Use of Harmful and Unlawful Fines and Fees. Growing out of the division's work in Ferguson, in March 2016, the division and Access to Justice issued a dear colleague letter to help state and local courts guard against excessive and unlawful fines and fees. The letter addresses some of the most common practices that run afoul of the U.S. Constitution and/or other federal laws, such as incarcerating individuals for nonpayment without determining their ability to pay. The letter also discusses the importance of due process protections such as notice and, in appropriate cases, the right to counsel; the need to avoid unconstitutional bail practices; and due process concerns raised by certain private probation arrangements. In November 2016, the department filed a statement of interest in a Virginia case, *Stinnie et al. v. Holcomb*, addressing the constitutionality of state policies that automatically suspend the driver's licenses of those who fail to pay court fines or fees.

"Justice must remain an undeniable right for all, not a special privilege for some."

– Head of the Civil Rights Division Vanita Gupta

Challenged Bail Practices that Result in the Punishment of Poverty. The division worked on the department's briefs in two bail cases – *Varden v. City of Clanton* in Alabama (February 2015) and *Walker v. City of Calhoun* in Georgia (August 2016) – arguing that if bail practices result in jailing people because of their poverty, without consideration of their ability to pay or alternatives to incarceration, such practices violate the Constitution. The division has also argued that these practices constitute bad public policy and may negatively impact public safety.

Filed Briefs to Support a Meaningful and Effective Right to Counsel. The division and the department's Office for Access to Justice filed briefs in cases around the country – including in

Washington, New York, Pennsylvania, Georgia and Idaho – arguing that Sixth Amendment violations can occur if public defenders can't talk confidentially with their client, investigate the allegations and meaningfully test the prosecution's case. In the New York case, *Hurrell-Harring v. State of New York*, just weeks after the department filed its statement of interest, New York reached a comprehensive settlement agreement with the plaintiffs to implement transformative reforms to its public defense system across five counties in the state. These reforms include guaranteeing that indigent criminal defendants will have legal counsel at arraignments and establishing caseload and workload standards for public defenders to ensure they can adequately serve each client. In the Pennsylvania case, *Kuren v. Luzerne County*, in September 2016, the Pennsylvania Supreme Court ruled that the systemic absence or compromise of traditional markers of representation and substantial structural limitations may constitute a constructive denial of counsel under the Sixth Amendment and allow defendants to seek prospective, injunctive relief.

Addressed the Criminalization of Homelessness. In an Idaho case, *Bell v. Boise*, the division filed a statement of interest in August 2015 arguing that because every human being must sleep at some time and in some place, arresting and punishing a person for sleeping in public – when there aren't enough shelter beds in the city and she has nowhere else to go – criminalizes the status of being homeless.

> "And this is our solemn obligation, as stewards of the law, and servants of those whom it protects and empowers: to open a frank and constructive dialogue about the need to reform a broken system. To fight for the sweeping, systemic changes we need. And to uphold our dearest values … by calling on our peers and colleagues not merely to serve their clients, or win their cases – but to ensure that – in every case, in every circumstance, and in every community – justice is done."
>
> *– Remarks from Attorney General Eric Holder at the 2013 Annual Meeting of the American Bar Association's House of Delegates*

ADVANCED JUVENILE JUSTICE REFORM

When young people end up serving time behind bars, rather than earning diplomas and landing jobs, that hurts us all. The harms and inequities in our juvenile justice system threaten to limit the opportunities and derail the futures of America's youth. For those children who end up in the juvenile justice system, the division works to ensure that they receive the full due process and equal protection rights our Constitution guarantees. The division has led investigations and reached settlements around the country to reform local juvenile justice systems.

Helped Drive Transformative Reforms in Ohio Juvenile Correctional Facilities. In December 2015, the division joined with the state of Ohio in seeking the termination of a consent decree with the Ohio Department of Youth Services (DYS), recognizing Ohio's successful elimination of its use of disciplinary solitary confinement on children in its custody and its improvement of individualized mental health treatment for children formerly at risk of such confinement. The court commended DYS for numerous improvements, including the abolition of the practice of disciplinary solitary confinement, its "vastly improved" mental health services and a reduction in the incarcerated population from over 2000 children to fewer than 500 today.

Entered into Agreement to Reform the Juvenile Court of Memphis and Shelby County, Tennessee. In December 2012, the division entered into a comprehensive memorandum of agreement with the Juvenile Court of Memphis and Shelby County, Tennessee, to resolve findings of serious and systemic failures in the juvenile court that violate children's due process and equal protection rights. This agreement marked the first time that the Justice Department has used its authority under the Violent Crime Control and Law Enforcement Act of 1994 to address constitutional violations within a juvenile justice system. The agreement aims to ensure that the juvenile court protects constitutional rights of children throughout their court proceedings. The agreement also requires the juvenile court to take steps to reduce racial disparities among similarly situated juveniles in different stages of the juvenile justice process. Enforcement of the agreement has led to the opening of a dedicated juvenile defense office in Memphis, significant reductions in the county's pre-adjudication detention population and a significant reduction in the number of juveniles transferred to the adult criminal court.

Entered into Agreement to Reform the Family Court of St. Louis County, Missouri. In December 2016, the division entered into a comprehensive agreement with the St. Louis County Family Court to resolve its findings of serious and systemic violations of juvenile due process and equal protection rights. The agreement aims to ensure that the family court protects the constitutional rights of children throughout their court proceedings and requires the family court to address racial disparities among youth in different stages of the juvenile justice process.

Reached Settlement Agreements to Address Unconstitutional Youth Arrest and Probation Practices in Meridian, Mississippi. In June 2015, the division, jointly with the state of Mississippi and city of Meridian, Mississippi, reached settlement agreements to prevent and address unconstitutional youth arrests and probation practices by the Meridian Police Department and the

<u>Mississippi Division of Youth Services</u>. In 2012, the division filed a lawsuit against the city of Meridian; the state of Mississippi; the Lauderdale County, Mississippi, Youth Court; and the Youth Court Judges, alleging systematic violations of youths' due process rights. The agreement with the city prevents police officers from arresting youth for behavior that is appropriately addressed as a school discipline issue, and requires documented probable cause determinations for any youth arrested for criminal offenses. The agreement with the state youth probation agency requires that staff notify children of their right to counsel at probation revocation hearings, among other protections.

Issued Guidance Package to Protect the Civil Rights of Students in Juvenile Justice Residential Facilities. In December 2014, the division joined with the U.S. Department of Education and <u>released a guidance package on juvenile correctional education</u>. The guidance included a dear colleague letter that established clear guidelines on how federal civil rights laws apply to the 60,000 youth in our country's juvenile justice residential facilities. The letter covered a range of areas, including equal opportunities to access academic coursework, administration of discipline and effective communication for students with disabilities, among others.

REFORMED RESTRICTIVE HOUSING AND CORRECTIONS PRACTICES

The division has worked for more than 20 years to end the abusive use of restrictive housing, including solitary confinement, in state and local prisons, jails and juvenile facilities. In recent years, the division has focused in particular on the unique harm that restrictive housing causes to vulnerable populations, such as prisoners with serious mental illness and juveniles. Under the Civil Rights of Institutionalized Persons Act (CRIPA), the division has the authority to investigate state and local jails and prisons to determine whether they are engaged in any patterns or practices that violate the rights of prisoners. If the division finds a pattern or practice of misconduct, it tries to negotiate a settlement agreement with the jurisdiction, most often in the form of a court-approved, independently-monitored consent decree. If these efforts fail, it has the authority to sue.

Issued Landmark Report with Proposed Reforms for Restrictive Housing. The division worked on the Justice Department's report, released in January 2016, which outlines a series of guiding principles for correctional systems across the country and detailed policy recommendations aimed to curtail and limit how the federal prison system uses restrictive housing, including solitary confinement. The report concluded that, "as a matter of policy, we believe strongly this practice should be used rarely, applied fairly and subjected to reasonable constraints." The recommendations for the Federal Bureau of Prisons (BOP) – which President Obama adopted – include ending solitary confinement for juveniles, diverting inmates with serious mental illness to secure mental health units and discouraging the placement of inmates in any form of restrictive housing during the final 180 days of their prison terms.

Ensured that Pennsylvania Department of Corrections Took Significant Steps to Reform its Use of Solitary Confinement. In April 2016, the division closed its investigation into the Pennsylvania Department of Corrections (PDOC) following significant improvements made by PDOC to its policies and practices that are intended to protect prisoners with serious mental illness and intellectual disabilities from the harmful effects of solitary confinement. The division opened its statewide investigation into the use of solitary confinement on prisoners with serious mental illness and intellectual disabilities in May 2013 after finding a pattern of constitutional violations as well as violations of the ADA at the State Correctional Institution in Cresson, Pennsylvania. In its closing letter to PDOC, the division noted that PDOC demonstrated its commitment to reforming its use of solitary confinement by working closely with the division and beginning improvements at the outset of the investigation. Since then, PDOC has worked to ensure that prisoners with serious mental illness and/or intellectual disabilities are no longer subjected to solitary confinement and are instead provided with specialized treatment to meet their individualized needs.

Reached Settlement to Reform Criminal Justice System in Hinds County, Mississippi. In June 2016, the division reached a landmark settlement agreement to reform the criminal justice system in Hinds County, Mississippi. The agreement resolves the division's findings that the Hinds County Adult Detention Center and the Jackson City Detention Center – which together form the

Hinds County Jail – failed to protect prisoners from violence and excessive force and held them past their court-ordered release dates, in violation of CRIPA. The settlement requires the county to implement a series of reforms across various stages of the criminal justice system, such as limiting the use of segregation and improving access to screening, treatment and community-based services for special needs prisoners, including juveniles and prisoners with serious mental illness. The settlement agreement is also the first of its kind to incorporate broader criminal justice system reform through diversion at the front end and reentry to the community after incarceration. It creates a criminal justice coordinating committee that will help ensure the county's systems operate effectively and efficiently; develop interventions to divert individuals in appropriate cases from arrest, detention and incarceration; and engage in community outreach.

PROTECTED THE RIGHTS OF LIMITED ENGLISH PROFICIENT (LEP) INDIVIDUALS AND PREVENTED NATIONAL ORIGIN AND RACIAL DISCRIMINATION BY RECIPIENTS OF FEDERAL FUNDS

Safeguarding access to justice requires ensuring that all people – regardless of where they come from or which language they speak – receive the full rights and protections they deserve. In 2010, the division launched a Courts Language Access Initiative to clarify that in compliance with Title VI of the Civil Rights Act of 1964, courts receiving federal financial assistance must provide meaningful access for limited English proficient (LEP) individuals. The division has also worked to train federal employees and provide them with the proper tools and resources to most effectively serve LEP populations. The Courts Language Access Initiative is just one example of the division's work to ensure that recipients of federal funds do not engage in any form of national origin and racial discrimination

Advanced Language Access in State Courts. Across the justice system, language access barriers can impede the ability of state courts to accurately evaluate facts and fairly administer justice. And they can also place unfair illegal burdens on individuals – from litigants, to defendants, to victims, to witnesses – who participate in court proceedings or seek assistance from court programs and services. Through a range of efforts, in states and jurisdictions across the country – including Maine; North Carolina; Rhode Island; Colorado; California; and King County, Washington – the division has worked to ensure that courts fully comply with their language access obligations. Since 2009, the division has worked with 23 state and local court systems to develop or improve policies to provide language services to individuals with limited English proficiency.

Worked with the New Jersey Department of Corrections to Improve Language Assistance Services for LEP Inmates. In October 2014, the division entered into an agreement to conclude a Title VI investigation based on complaints filed by LEP inmates who alleged they were subject to national origin discrimination. The agreement includes new policies and procedures to improve access to language assistance services for LEP inmates in New Jersey.

Reached Agreement with Washington State Department of Labor and Industries to Improve Access for LEP Workers. In October 2015, the division and the U.S. Department of Labor reached an agreement with the Washington State Department of Labor and Industries to resolve civil rights complaints from LEP individuals who alleged that they were subject to national origin discrimination in the state's workers' compensation program. These complainants alleged that they were denied access to interpreters and to vital information in their primary languages in workers' compensation investigations and enforcement proceedings. The agreement calls for significant improvements in language assistance services for LEP individuals.

Helped Make Federal Agencies Accessible to LEP Individuals. In April 2015, the division-chaired Interagency Working Group on Limited English Proficiency (IWG) produced an interactive video training series for federal personnel on interactions with LEP individuals and non-English speakers. The IWG developed this video training series in response to the Attorney General's February 2011 memorandum to all federal agencies reaffirming the administration's commitment to the language access principles of Executive Order 13166.

Released Mapping and Procurement Resources to Help Federal and Federally-Funded Agencies Determine and Respond to the Needs of LEP Individuals. In August 2015, the division publically launched its first mapping application and related maps. The Language Map App is an interactive demographic map that uses the U.S. Census 2008-2012 American Community Survey (ACS) 5-Year Estimate data to show the number and concentration of LEP individuals in the United States by language. Paired with the division's Translation and Interpretation Procurement Series (TIPS) resources released in 2014, the Map App and TIPS resources enable and enhance the ability of federal and federally-funded agencies to respond to the needs of LEP individuals, in compliance with Title VI and Executive Order 13166. Together, the training series, the Language Map App and the TIPS enhance the ability of federal employees to communicate accurately with LEP individuals.

Issued Joint Guidance for Child Welfare Systems About Civil Rights Laws and Child Welfare Systems. In October 2016, the division and the U.S. Department of Health and Human Services (HHS) issued a joint guidance letter to state and local child welfare systems on the requirements of Title VI and its implementing regulations. The guidance aims to ensure that child welfare systems know about their responsibilities to protect the civil rights of children and families. Among other matters, the 2016 guidance letter addresses race and national origin discrimination that may lead to unnecessary removal of children from their biological families and denial of full participation in family courts and social services. In 2015, the departments issued guidance on the intersection of child welfare requirements and Title II of the Americans with Disabilities Act and Section 504 of the Rehabilitation Act.

Issued Joint Guidance to Help Emergency Preparedness, Response and Recovery Providers Comply with Title VI of the Civil Rights Act. The division released joint guidance in August 2016, along with the Departments of Health and Human Services, Housing and Urban Development, Homeland Security and Transportation to help ensure that recipients of federal financial assistance do not discriminate against individuals and communities based on race, color or nation origin when providing emergency preparedness, response and recovery services. Title VI prohibits discrimination based on race, color or national origin in federally-funded programs or activities. The guidance suggests a series of steps recipients can adopt to ensure compliance.

Led Community Outreach to Asian Americans and Pacific Islanders to Better Understand Challenges Facing Vulnerable Worker Populations. Through the Justice Department's participation in the White House Initiative on Asian Americans and Pacific Islanders, the division designed and launched the Vulnerable Workers Project (VWP) Interagency Working Group, which hosted listening sessions with Asian American and Pacific Islander (AAPI) workers and their advocates in multiple U.S. cities, composed a report summarizing the concerns raised during the listening sessions and advanced recommendations for federal agencies to address these concerns and further support AAPI workers.

Filed Brief to Protect the Rights of Refugees. When Indiana declared that it would not permit federal grant funds to be spent on social services for Syrian refugees who had immigrated into the state, the division worked on the Justice Department's brief taking the position that this action could violate the 14th Amendment's equal protection clause, Title VI and the terms of the Refugee Act of 1980. In its brief, the department explained that "The long-established policy and practice of the United States is to welcome vulnerable refugees who have suffered persecution to the country, offer them safe haven, and help them build new lives and ultimately become self-sufficient, all while maintaining the national security of the United States."

RESOURCES

Reports and Publications:

- The Civil Rights Division's Pattern and Practice Police Reform Work: 1994 – Present and Interactive Police Reform Finder (January 2017)

- Advancing Diversity in Law Enforcement (October 2016)

- Language Access in State Courts (September 2016)

- Combating Religious Discrimination Today: Final Report (July 2016)

- Update on the Justice Department's Enforcement of the Religious Land Use and Institutionalized Persons Act: 2010 –2016 (July 2016)

- Beyond the Cases: 26 Years of the Americans with Disabilities Act: The Lives, Faces, and Stories Behind the ADA (July 2016)

- U.S. Department of Justice Report and Recommendations Concerning the Use of Restrictive Housing (January 2016)

- Report on the Tenth Anniversary of the Trafficking Victims Protection Act (October 2010)

- Civil Rights Division Accomplishments for 2009-2012 and 2013

Newsletters:

- Religious Freedom in Focus
  The division publishes a periodic email update about its religious liberty and religious discrimination cases.

- OSC Update
  The division's Office of Special Counsel for Immigration-related Unfair Employment Practices publishes a quarterly newsletter highlighting the section's work.

- Title VI Civil Rights News @ FCS
  The division's Federal Coordination and Compliance Section publishes a quarterly newsletter highlighting Title VI enforcement efforts.

Guidance and Technical Assistance:

- RLUIPA Letter to Mayors and Other Local Officials (December 2016)

- Statement of the Department of Justice on Application of the Integration Mandate of Title II of the Americans with Disabilities Act and *Olmstead v. L.C.* to State and Local

Governments' Employment Service Systems for Individuals with Disabilities (October (2016)

- Joint Guidance to Help Schools Ensure the Civil Rights of Transgender Students (May 2016)

- Dear Colleague Letter Regarding Law Enforcement Fines and Fees (March 2016)

- Identifying and Preventing Gender Bias in Law Enforcement Response to Sexual Assault and Domestic Violence (December 2015)

www.ingramcontent.com/pod-product-compliance
Lightning Source LLC
Chambersburg PA
CBHW081424280526
45788CB00009B/3217

* 9 7 8 1 5 4 2 6 7 0 3 8 8 *